CW01659445

Agile Project Framework

DSDM®
CONSORTIUM

Published by the DSDM Consortium

First printed August 2014   ISBN 978-0-9928727-0-0

Reprinted March 2016

For further information regarding this and other DSDM products please contact:

DSDM Consortium
Henwood House
Henwood
Ashford, Kent
TN24 8DH, United Kingdom

Website: www.dsdm.org

Printed in the United Kingdom by Buckland Media Group Limited, www.buckland.co.uk

Acknowledgements
Editorial Team: Andrew Craddock, Barbara Roberts, Dan Martland, Dorothy Tudor, Jennifer Stapleton, Julia Godwin, Keith Richards, Mark Buchan and Steve Messenger

Production: Emily Ruffle, Kim Whitmore, Mary Henson with artwork by Debbie Cole Creative Marketing

Contents

Introduction 3
The DSDM Agile Project Framework (AgilePF) 5
How does DSDM differ from more traditional approaches 6
How does DSDM differ from most Agile approaches? 6
Why choose DSDM Agile PF as your Agile approach? 7
More on the Values in the Agile Manifesto 8
Philosophy and Fundamentals 11
The DSDM Principles 15
Process 18
Roles and Responsibilities 22
Products 28
Project Planning and Control 35
The DSDM Practices 39
In Summary 50

Foreword

In recent years, as Agile becomes more and more popular, organisations have seen that some circumstances actually benefit from a combination of different Agile approaches, allowing them to build on the strengths of individual Agile styles – sometimes called "blended Agile". DSDM® is proving very popular here, as it is one of the few Agile approaches that has always focused on delivering Agile Projects, and this is the biggest area of growth in the take-up of Agile.

This move towards blended Agile is reflected in the latest version of DSDM – the Agile Project Framework – the first product to support DSDM's future strategy. In Agile Project Framework a number of links out to other Agile approaches are identified by a link logo :

The Agile Project Framework 2014 provides the information needed by any role working on a DSDM project, whether technical, business or management. DSDM will support this framework by a number of role-specific guides, which focus on the additional information needed by other roles working on an Agile project, e.g. an Agile Business Analyst or an Agile Project Manager.

This pocket book provides a summary of information contained in the Handbook, and outlines the topics that define the foundation of DSDM. For more information, please see www.dsdm.org or The Agile Project Framework Handbook

Barbara Roberts
DSDM Director for Product Innovation

Introduction

DSDM and the DSDM Consortium

DSDM® is a proven framework for Agile project management and solution delivery, helping to deliver business value quickly and effectively. It has been applied to a wide range of projects - from small business systems developments and enhancements all the way up to full-scale business change projects.

In 1994, when DSDM was created, the world of solution delivery through projects was very different from how it is today. The corporate world predominantly used a traditional 'Waterfall' approach for their projects – an approach that was first defined and adopted in the early 1970s.

Far too many projects were failing by running over time, over budget and fundamentally failing to deliver a solution that genuinely met the need of the sponsoring business. This was largely because projects were too big and too long and were made artificially complex by trying to deal with *all* the immediate needs (however trivial) as well as trying to meet future needs that could only be guessed at. Communication and business engagement were poor and progress was measured in terms of how much of the planned work had been done rather than how much business value had been delivered.

To counter these problems, some projects had tried a completely different approach – Rapid Application Development (RAD) – with users of a proposed computer system working closely with developers to iteratively and incrementally build software applications, based on discussions, demonstrations and short feedback loops, rather than formalised up-front specifications. RAD addressed many of the problems of the traditional approach but, in doing so, it introduced a whole new set of problems, particularly around the supportability and scalability of the solutions. This was because the *disciplines* of analysis and design were thrown out with the up-front Waterfall phases that used to contain them.

The founding members of the DSDM Consortium, representing a spectrum of companies from large multinationals to small businesses and from both customer and supplier organisations, recognised that both approaches had strengths and areas for improvement. They worked together to bring the best parts from the traditional approach (control and quality) and from RAD (good communication, business collaboration, transparency) to create a new, holistic approach to project management and delivery.

In 2001 the DSDM Consortium helped shape the Manifesto for Agile Software Development, to create the Agile Alliance and thus to change the software project landscape to support the fast-changing worlds of business and technology in the 21st century. The manifesto states:

> We are uncovering better ways of developing software
> by doing it and helping others do it.
> Through this work we have come to value:
>
> **Individuals and interactions over** processes and tools
> **Customer collaboration over** contract negotiation
> **Working software over** comprehensive documentation
> **Responding to change over** following a plan
>
> That is, while there is value in the items on the right,
> we value the items on the left more.

Where more complex, more regulated project environments require stronger governance and control, DSDM recognises that additional emphasis on the items on the right may be necessary, but that a fully Agile project is still possible.

The DSDM Agile Project Framework (AgilePF)

AgilePF™ is an evolution of Atern®, the previous version of DSDM. It describes everything required to enable anybody involved in a DSDM project to use the framework to deliver projects on time, on budget and to the agreed level of quality every time.

AgilePF retains DSDM's project-focused principles, together with its rich set of roles and responsibilities that are ideally suited to a corporate project environment. It also continues to embrace the same robust and fully Agile DSDM practices for establishing and demonstrating control in a project.

At the delivery level, the DSDM process has been simplified to better reflect current trends in evolutionary solution development. The most significant change is in the area of the products, or deliverables, associated with the process. Although the level of formality and indeed inclusion or exclusion of individual products has always been discretionary, the latest product set has been streamlined to align more obviously with the Agile philosophy to keep essential documentation lean, timely and valuable.

From late 2014, in line with a strategic objective to continue to provide depth and breadth of guidance for Agile project practitioners, DSDM's Agile Project Management (AgilePM®) will be based on AgilePF and provide additional guidance for Project Managers. Around the same time Agile Business Analysis (AgileBA®), also based on AgilePF, will launch and provide depth and detail of guidance for Business Analysts working in an Agile project environment.

How does DSDM differ from traditional approaches?

In DSDM, the iterative approach encourages the emergence of detail over time; therefore, the current step needs to be completed in only enough detail to allow the project to move to the next step with any shortfall in detailed understanding being dealt with in a subsequent iteration of development. Given the strong probability that business requirements will change over time, and that such change is most likely to happen at the detail level, the effort traditionally spent on trying to document the detail of all requirements up-front is avoided in DSDM. Solutions built using the DSDM approach address the current and imminent needs of the business, leaving potential future needs for consideration closer to that time.

As a result, solutions are more likely to have a better fit with the true business need and are easier to test and easier to integrate into existing and emerging business processes. The development cost of most solutions is only a small part of the total cost of ownership; it therefore makes sense to build simpler solutions that are both fit for purpose on the day of delivery and easier to maintain and modify thereafter. This is preferable to trying to implement a more extensive solution that has been complicated and often compromised by failed attempts to predict future business needs.

How does DSDM differ from most Agile approaches?

DSDM is a 'whole project' approach. It requires basic foundations for the project to be agreed at an early stage and allows detail to emerge over time. Establishing firm foundations allows businesses to understand the scope and fundamental characteristics of the proposed solution, and the way it will be created, before development starts. Clarifying and agreeing the foundations for the project from the combined perspectives of business, solution and management reduces the likelihood of nasty surprises on DSDM projects.

For larger corporate organisations or those with a complex architecture or governance standards, agreeing the foundations early in the project is essential.

DSDM also describes a broader set of roles than most Agile approaches giving it a better fit with most corporate environments but without compromising Agility.

Why choose DSDM AgilePF as your Agile approach

DSDM has a broader focus than most other Agile approaches in that it deals with projects rather than just the development and delivery of a product (typically software). The project context requires a focus on the wider business need and all aspects of the solution that evolves to meet that need.

DSDM may also be used to supplement an existing in-house Agile approach, where this has proved to be lacking in some way. For example, DSDM is often used to provide the *full project* focus to complement Scrum's team-focused product development process. The Agile Project Management and Scrum pocketbook provides guidance on this particular combination.

Although DSDM provides a robust mechanism for project governance and control, where needed, it can also be easily tailored to work alongside other standards and approaches, for example with PRINCE2®, PMI and ITIL. DSDM has also been proven to operate effectively within formal quality frameworks such as ISO 9001 and CMMI.

More on the values in the Agile Manifesto

Individuals and interactions over processes and tools

In an Agile project, great emphasis is placed on the team. Every individual in the team is expected to be ready, willing and able to play their part in the project, carrying out their role with competence and professionalism. Every member of the team is expected to work collaboratively with everybody else, using his or her knowledge, experience and judgement to shape a project outcome that best meets the need of the sponsoring business. Processes and tools play an important part in any project but much less emphasis is placed on these in an Agile environment. Agile processes need to be light touch and serve to guide and support rather than dictate what individuals and teams do and how they should do it. The assumption is that the team is best placed to understand what needs to be done and to work out the best way of doing it. DSDM provides appropriate light touch guidance on roles and responsibilities, whilst keeping the emphasis at all times on the people and the way they work together.

Working software over comprehensive documentation

The choice of words used here reflects the origins and primary focus of Agile – a focus solely on software delivery. However, changing a single word – 'software' to 'solution' - elevates this value from delivery of a software product to encompass the broader context of business change projects and often this is the interpretation for DSDM. DSDM has been proven to work equally well for both software and non-software projects.

The message behind this Agile value is to break the illusion of security and stability that comes from document-driven processes. Specification of every detail of requirements, solution design, plans etc. in documents that get 'signed off' by stakeholders before work is allowed to progress is both wasteful and ineffective. DSDM embraces the need for high-level versions of these artefacts in the early phases to frame development and delivery projects and to support governance. After the Foundations phase in a project, the framework employs collaborative practices with active business engagement to ensure that the right solution is delivered. The framework also advocates light and timely documentation to support the solution in production beyond the end of the project.

Customer collaboration over contract negotiation

This Agile value encourages project teams and the sponsoring business to work collaboratively at all times. Typical commercial contracts assume that a traditional Waterfall process underpins development and 'a fixed price for a fixed specification' is the standard for project contracts. Agile projects emphasise collaboration, and therefore contracts need to reflect this.

A contract can be as formal as a document signed by those responsible for sponsoring the solution and by those delivering it, or as informal as a shared verbal agreement on what is to be delivered. Regardless of formality, it is important to ensure that, where created, all parties follow the principle of such documents or agreements being 'light touch' and 'guiding' rather than being 'detailed' and 'prescriptive'. By this definition, DSDM's Prioritised Requirements List may represent a contract, effectively defining the scope of a project. However, as it is at a high level, it requires customer collaboration with less formality to expand on the detail of requirements throughout the iterative development of the solution during the project lifecycle.

Responding to change over following a plan

This Agile value emphasises the fact that the world around a project is rarely frozen in time. Change occurs so quickly in the world of business now that adopting an approach to building a solution which accommodates, or ideally embraces, change is likely to be the only way to a successful outcome. Change may also arise as a result of an emerging understanding of what is needed, what is valuable and even what is possible. The degree of change in detail that is typical of most projects makes creating detailed, long-term plans a waste of time. Where change is normal rather than the exception, the high-level 'light touch' and 'guiding' plans advocated by DSDM better meet the need of a flexible business.

And the very important final sentence

DSDM specifically embraces the last sentence in the Agile Manifesto that clearly states, in the context of the values above:

> ***"That is, while there is value in the items on the right, we value the items on the left more."***

It is important not to ignore processes, tools, documentation, contracts and plans but instead to ensure that they are only created where they add value, and only to the level of detail that adds value. They should be created in a form relevant to and taking full advantage of the Agile values.

Philosophy and Fundamentals

Introduction

The DSDM philosophy is that

"best business value emerges when projects are aligned to clear business goals, deliver frequently and involve the collaboration of motivated and empowered people."

This is achieved when all stakeholders:

- Understand and buy into the business vision and objectives
- Are empowered to make decisions within their area of expertise
- Collaborate to deliver a fit for purpose business solution
- Collaborate to deliver to agreed timescales in accordance with business priorities
- Accept that change is inevitable as the understanding of the solution grows over time

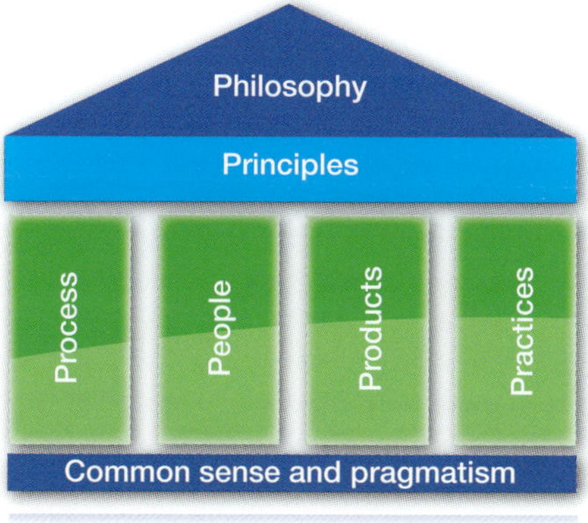

The DSDM philosophy is supported by a set of eight principles that build the mindset and behaviours necessary to bring the philosophy alive. The principles are themselves supported by people (with defined roles and responsibilities), an Agile process (enabling an iterative and incremental lifecycle to shape development and delivery), clearly defined products and recommended practices to help achieve the optimum results.

DSDM's approach and style has always been founded on an underlying ethos of common sense and pragmatism. It may be useful to clarify the meaning of these words:

Common sense - "sound practical judgment independent of specialised knowledge or training; normal native intelligence."

Pragmatism - "action or policy dictated by consideration of the immediate practical consequences rather than by theory or dogma."

Common sense and pragmatism underpin "the way DSDM works", helping to avoid the dogma that is sometimes encountered in the world of Agile and ensuring that "individuals and interactions" continue to take precedence over "processes and tools".

Understanding project variables

Projects have to balance conflicting demands, and the four most common demands are: time; cost; features to be delivered and quality. Experience shows that trying to fix all four of these at the outset of a project is unrealistic and common sense suggests that we should not try. Conversely, pragmatism dictates that at least some of these should be fixed so that a project can be properly controlled and governed. Organisations willing to accept that 'something good will be delivered at some point for a reasonable amount of money' are not very common. The desire to fix everything is, however, much more common and is the cause of many project failures because there is rarely sufficient contingency to allow for the high degree of change that results from a poor collective understanding of requirements and their implications in terms of development and business impact.

For this reason, it is important at the start of a project to ask the question "If we hit a problem, what do we protect (fix) and what can we negotiate (vary) if necessary?"

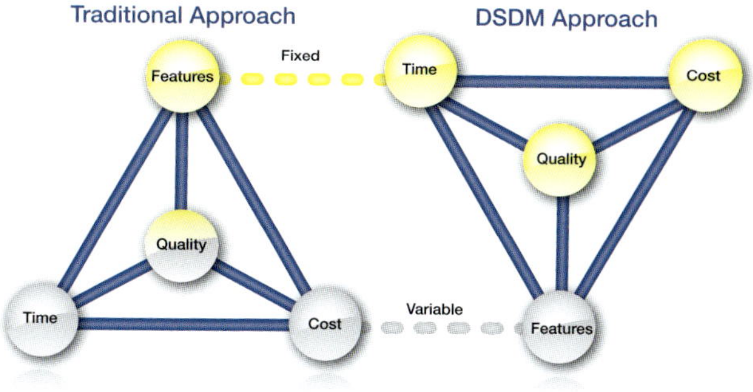

Typically, in the **traditional approach** to managing a project (to the left in the diagram), the feature content of the solution is fixed whilst time and cost are subject to variation. Quality also tends to become an unplanned variable primarily due to the fact that testing is typically left to the end of the project and, as a result of an attempt to make up for previous overruns, is either truncated in terms of testing effort or the time available to fix any defects identified.

By default, **the DSDM approach** to managing the project (to the right of the diagram) fixes time, cost and quality at the end of the Foundations phase while contingency is managed by varying the features (the requirements) to be delivered. As and when contingency is required, the business roles identify the least valuable of the remaining requirements that are then dropped or deferred in order to keep the project on track.

A DSDM project will always deliver a viable solution, on time and on cost (on budget), as long as the practices of MoSCoW and Timeboxing are followed. Delivery of a Minimum Usable SubseT of requirements is guaranteed as a worst case scenario. However, in all but the most extreme circumstances, the expectation is to deliver far more than the bare minimum.

The iterative and incremental approach to development ensures that the more important requirements are built to the agreed level of quality. Only once this has been achieved does development start on the less important requirements. Incremental delivery of the Evolving Solution ensures that, on the day that the solution is deployed into live use, quality is at the level expected and previously agreed.

Summary

To bring to life the philosophy that *"best business value emerges when projects are aligned to clear business goals, deliver frequently and involve the collaboration of motivated and empowered people"*, DSDM offers a framework of eight principles, supported by definition of, and guidance on, people, products, process and practices (all of which are described in the following sections). All of this guidance needs to be applied with common sense and pragmatism; adapting to the project's environment and context, while preserving the philosophy of DSDM Agility.

The DSDM Principles

DSDM defines eight principles that help shape projects and guide project teams in making them successful. Compromising any of the principles undermines the philosophy of DSDM and introduces risk to the successful outcome of the project. If a team doesn't follow all of these principles then it won't get the full benefit of the approach. The collective application of DSDM's principles brings the philosophy to life.

The eight principles are:

Principle 1 - Focus on the Business Need

Every decision taken during a project should be viewed in the light of the overriding project goal - to deliver what the business needs to be delivered, when it needs to be delivered.

Principle 2 - Deliver on Time

Delivering a solution on time is a very desirable outcome for a project and is quite often the single most important success factor. Late delivery can often undermine the very rationale for a project, especially where market opportunities or legal deadlines are involved. Even where this is not the case, on-time delivery of intermediate or contributing products is still the best way to demonstrate control over the project.

Principle 3 – Collaborate

Teams that work in a spirit of active cooperation and commitment will always outperform groups of individuals working only in loose association. Collaboration encourages increased understanding, greater speed and shared ownership, which enable teams to perform at a level that exceeds the sum of their parts.

Principle 4 - Never Compromise Quality

In DSDM, the level of quality to be delivered should be agreed at the start. All work should be aimed at achieving that level of quality - no more and no less. A solution has to be 'good enough'. If the business agrees that the features in the Minimum Usable SubseT meet the agreed acceptance criteria, then the solution should be 'good enough' to use.

Principle 5 - Build Incrementally from Firm Foundations

One of the key differentiators for DSDM within the Agile space is the concept of establishing firm foundations for the project before committing to significant development. DSDM advocates first understanding the scope of the business problem to be solved and the proposed solution, but not in such detail that the project becomes paralysed by overly detailed analysis of requirements.

Once firm foundations for development have been established, DSDM advocates incremental delivery of the solution in order to deliver real business benefit as early as is practical. Incremental delivery encourages stakeholder confidence, offering a source of feedback for use in subsequent Timeboxes and may lead to the early realisation of business benefit.

Principle 6 - Develop Iteratively

DSDM uses a combination of Iterative Development, frequent demonstrations and comprehensive review to encourage timely feedback. Embracing change as part of this evolutionary process allows the team to converge on an accurate business solution. The concept of iteration is at the heart of everything developed as part of the DSDM approach. It is very rare that anything is created perfectly first time and it is important to recognise that projects operate within a changing world.

Principle 7 - Communicate Continuously and Clearly

Poor communication is often cited as the biggest single cause of project failure. DSDM practices are specifically designed to improve communication effectiveness for both teams and individuals.

Principle 8 - Demonstrate Control

It is essential to be in control of a project at all times and to be able to demonstrate that this is the case. This can only be achieved by reference to a plan for the work being done, which is clearly aligned with agreed business objectives. It is also vital to ensure transparency of all work being performed by the team.

Summary

The eight principles help direct and shape the attitude and mindset of a DSDM team. Compromising any of the principles undermines DSDM's philosophy, as together they deliver a collective value that outweighs their individual benefits.

Process

Overview

The DSDM approach to development and delivery is both iterative and incremental, with the most important business needs typically being addressed early while less important features are delivered later.

Unlike most Agile approaches, DSDM integrates project management and product development into a single process.

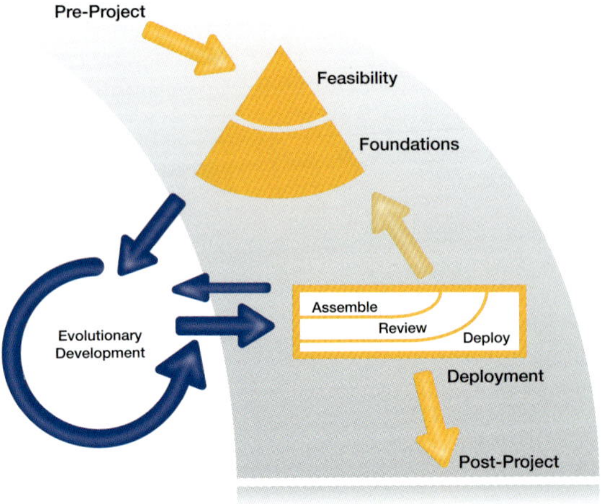

Pre-Project Phase

The Pre-Project phase ensures that only the right projects are started, and that they are set up correctly, based on a clearly defined objective.

Feasibility Phase

The Feasibility phase is intended primarily to establish whether the proposed project is likely to be feasible from a technical perspective and whether it appears cost-effective from a business perspective. The effort associated with Feasibility should be just enough to decide whether further investigation is justified, or whether the project should be stopped now, as it is unlikely to be viable.

Foundations Phase

The Foundations phase takes the preliminary investigation from Feasibility to the next level. It is intended to establish a fundamental (but not detailed) understanding of the business rationale for the project, the potential solution that will be created by the project, and how development and delivery of the solution will be managed.

The aim of Foundations is to understand the scope of work, and in broad terms, how it will be carried out, by whom, when and where. The detail associated with requirements, and how they should be met as part of the solution, is intentionally left until the Evolutionary Development phase of the project.

For smaller, simpler projects, the Feasibility and Foundations phases can often be merged into a single phase. For larger, more complex projects, it may sometimes be necessary to revisit Foundations after each Deployment phase.

Evolutionary Development Phase

Building on the firm foundations that have been established for the project, the purpose of the Evolutionary Development phase is to evolve the solution.

The Evolutionary Development phase requires the Solution Development Team(s) to apply practices such as Iterative Development, Timeboxing, and MoSCoW prioritisation, together with Modelling and Facilitated Workshops, to converge over time on an accurate solution that meets the business need and is also built in the right way from a technical viewpoint.

Working within Timeboxes, the Solution Development Team create Solution Increments, iteratively exploring the low-level detail of the requirements and testing continuously as they move forward.

Deployment Phase

The objective of the Deployment phase is to bring a baseline of the Evolving Solution into operational use. The release that is deployed may be the final solution, or a subset of the final solution.

The Deployment phase comprises three main activities: Assemble, Review and Deploy. In addition, after the last release, the project is formally closed.

Post-Project Phase

After the final Deployment for a project, the Post-Project phase checks how well the expected business benefits have been met.

The Lifecycle in Practice

Whilst there is a clear progression of phases from Pre-Project to Post-Project in the process diagram above, there are also arrows indicating a return path within the process that allow a project-specific lifecycle to be agreed at the end of Foundations to support Iterative Development and incremental delivery of the Evolving Solution.

Configuring DSDM for Scalability and Formality

DSDM recognises the real value of Agility in terms of project productivity and solution quality while acknowledging and accepting the necessary constraints that often exist when working in a corporate environment. Such constraints may include financial governance, architecture and/or infrastructure strategies, regulatory governance, vendor agreements and third party support considerations.

The DSDM process can be configured and calibrated to cater for a range of projects from small projects with light governance to larger projects with stronger governance needs. Typically this is achieved by configuring a lifecycle appropriate for a specific project and determining an appropriate level of formality with which the DSDM products are defined, created and approved.

With regards to scaling, the project organisation can easily be refined to support multiple teams, with key roles acting as directors and coordinators across the teams. To support a more complex project structure, products such as the Solution Architecture Definition, Development Approach Definition, Management Approach Definition and the Delivery Plan and Timebox Review Records can be made more elaborate and more formal than would be appropriate for smaller projects.

Summary

Through the tailoring of its various products, and the responsibilities associated with project-level roles, the DSDM Agile Project Framework ensures the iterative and incremental approach to solution delivery is appropriately and demonstrably coordinated and controlled regardless of project size and complexity.

Roles and Responsibilities

Introduction

People working together effectively are the foundation of any successful project. DSDM recognises this and assigns clear roles and responsibilities to each person in a project.

The best solutions emerge from self-organising, empowered teams. However, these teams, and the people within them, must actively take on the responsibility for their empowerment within the boundaries that have been agreed and collaborate fully to meet the real needs of the business.

In the diagram below

- Orange – identifies roles representing Business interests
- Green – identifies roles representing Solution development
- Blue – identifies roles representing Management interests
- Grey – identifies roles with specific process interests
- Mix of two colours – identifies a combined interest

It also differentiates between:

- Project-level roles – with responsibility for directing and coordinating the work undertaken by one or more Solution Development Teams
- Solution Development Team roles – responsible day-to-day for all the work required to build the solution
- Supporting roles – providing assistance and guidance to the project on an ad hoc basis throughout the lifecycle

All roles at the project level need to adopt the facilitative, empowering leadership style which allows Agile teams to learn as they go, getting to an end point by their own means, within an agreed framework of empowerment.

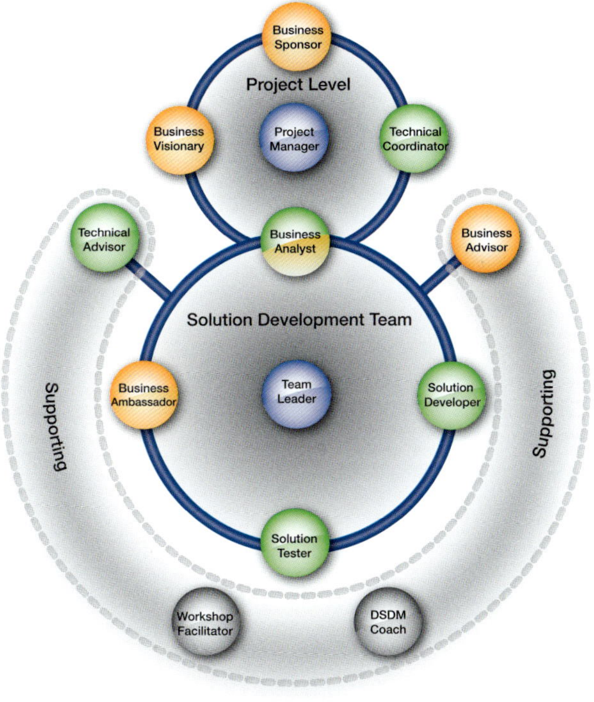

One DSDM role does not necessarily mean one person. One person may take on one or more roles. One role may be shared by two or more people. Where a role is shared it is vital that the individuals communicate and collaborate closely.

Role descriptions

Business Sponsor

This role is the most senior project-level business role. The Business Sponsor is the project champion who is committed to the project, to the proposed solution and the approach to delivering it. The Business Sponsor is specifically responsible for the Business Case and project budget throughout (however formally or informally this may be expressed).

Business Visionary

This is a senior project-level business role that should be held by a single individual, since a project needs a single clear vision to avoid confusion and misdirection. More actively involved than the Business Sponsor, the Business Visionary provides the team with strategic direction and ensures that the solution delivered will enable the benefits described in the Business Case to be achieved.

Technical Coordinator

As the project's technical authority, the Technical Coordinator ensures that the solution/technical roles work in a consistent way, that the project is technically coherent and meets the desired technical standards. The Technical Coordinator performs the same function from a technical perspective as the Business Visionary does from a business perspective.

Project Manager

As well as providing high-level Agile-style leadership to the Solution Development Team, the role is focused on managing the working environment in which the solution is evolving. The Project Manager also coordinates all aspects of management of the project at a high level but, in line with the DSDM concept of empowerment, the Project Manager is expected to leave the detailed planning of the actual delivery of the product(s) to the members of the Solution Development Team. Managing an empowered team requires a facilitative style rather than a 'command and control' style.

Business Analyst

The Business Analyst is both active in supporting the project-level roles and fully integrated with the Solution Development Team. The Business Analyst facilitates the relationship between the business and technical roles, ensuring accurate and appropriate decisions are made on the Evolving Solution on a day-to-day basis. The Business Analyst ensures that the business needs are properly analysed and understood by the all members of the Solution Development Team. The Business Analyst never replaces the business roles and **never** acts as an intermediary between Business and Solution roles but, instead, supports and facilitates the communication between them.

Business Ambassador

The Business Ambassador is embedded within the Solution Development Team as the key representative of and decision maker for the business. Responsible for providing the day-to-day detail of the requirements as development progresses and acknowledging that the Evolving Solution will meet the needs of the business, the Business Ambassador needs to be fully aware of and bought into the business vision and empowered to ensure the solution contributes properly to that vision.

Solution Developer

The Solution Developer collaborates with the other Solution Development Team roles to interpret business requirements and translate them into a Solution Increment that meets functional and non-functional needs of the business as a whole.

Solution Tester

The Solution Tester is an empowered Solution Development Team role, fully integrated with the team and performing testing throughout the project in accordance with the agreed strategy.

Business Advisor

As a business subject matter expert, the Business Advisor is called upon to provide specific, and often specialist, input to solution development or solution testing. The Business Advisor may be an intended user or beneficiary of the solution or may, for example, provide legal or regulatory advice with which the solution must comply.

Technical Advisor

The Technical Advisor supports the team by providing specific, and often specialist, technical input to the project, often from the perspective of those responsible for operational change management, operational support, ongoing maintenance of the solution, etc.

Team Leader

The Team Leader ideally acts as the servant-leader for the Solution Development Team and ensures that it functions as a whole and meets its objectives. The Team Leader works with the team to plan and coordinate all aspects of product delivery at the detailed level. As a part-time leadership (not management) role it is likely that the Team Leader will also fulfill another Solution Development Team role such as a Solution Developer or Solution Tester.

Workshop Facilitator

The Workshop Facilitator is responsible for planning, organizing and facilitating workshops to ensure that a group of people collaborates to meet a predetermined objective in a compressed timeframe. The Workshop Facilitator should ideally be independent of the outcome to be achieved in the workshop.

DSDM Coach

Where a team has limited experience of using DSDM, the role of the DSDM Coach is key to helping team members to get the most out of the approach, within the context and constraints of the wider organisation in which they work.

Summary

DSDM identifies roles and defines responsibilities for everybody with a part to play in a DSDM project, whether as a director and coordinator of the project (the project-level roles) or as a participant in the collaborative development of the solution (the Solution development Team roles). Business, solution development and project management interests are all represented along with roles intended to support the DSDM process. Active engagement of the business representatives and collaboration across all roles ensure that the optimum business solution emerges, built to the right level of quality and within the agreed time and budgetary constraints.

Products

DSDM describes a set of products to be considered as the project proceeds. These products include the solution itself (the main deliverable of the project), anything created to help with the process of evolving it, and anything required to help with project governance and control.

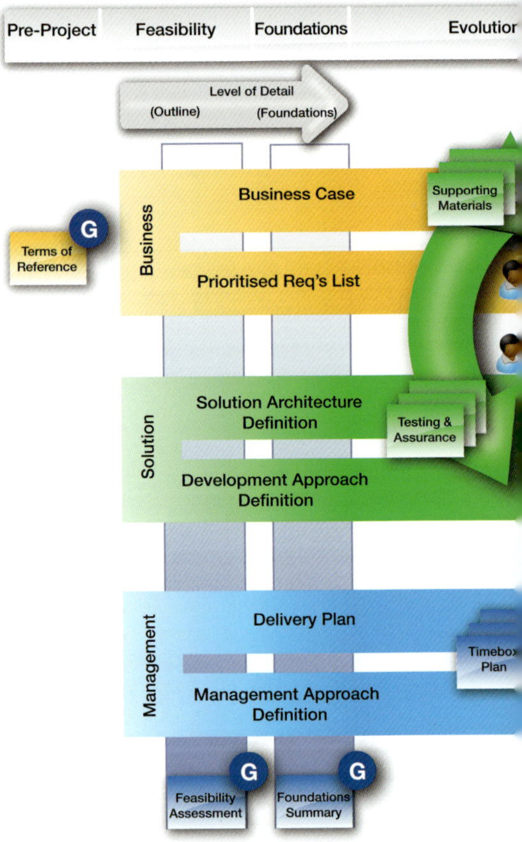

Not all products are required for every project and the formality associated with each product will vary from project to project and from organisation to organisation. The formality of the products is influenced by factors such as contractual relationships, corporate standards and governance needs.

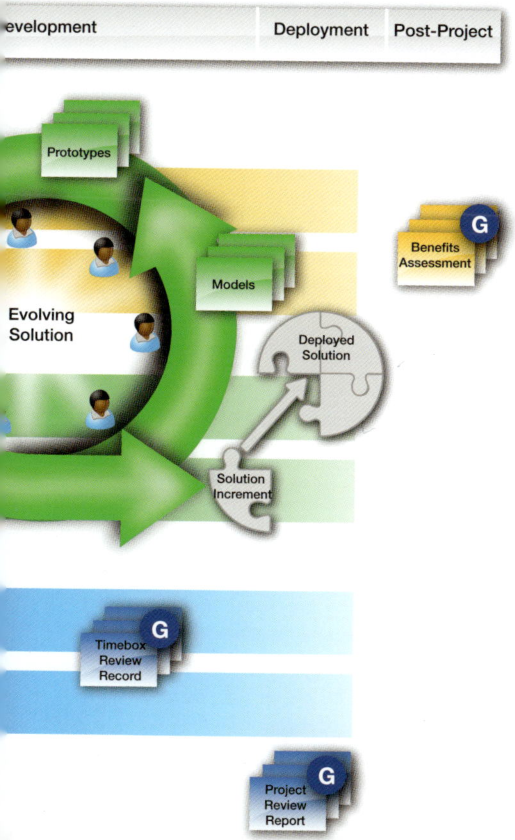

The products, and where they feature in the project lifecycle, are shown in the diagram above. Orange products are business-focused, green products all contribute to the solution being created by the project and blue products cover project management/control interests.

Several of the products - those marked with G - may also play a part in governance processes such as approval gateways, and may be used to demonstrate compliance of the solution with corporate and regulatory standards where this is required.

Terms of Reference

The Terms of Reference is a high-level definition of the over-arching business driver for, and top-level objectives of, the project. The primary aim of the Terms of Reference is to scope and justify the Feasibility phase. It is identified as a governance product because it may be used for purposes such as prioritisation of a project within a portfolio.

Business Case

The Business Case provides a vision of the business at the end of the project and a business justification for the investment of effort and other resources that make up a project. Baselines of the Business Case are typically created first as an outline by the end of Feasibility, then as a basis for approval of development by the end of Foundations.

Prioritised Requirements List

The Prioritised Requirement List (PRL) describes, at a high level, the requirements that the project needs to address and indicates their priority with respect to meeting the needs of the business. Consideration of requirements begins in Feasibility and a baseline of the PRL describes the scope of the project as at the end of Foundations. It is expected that the requirements will continue to be refined for depth and detail as the project proceeds with change to the high-level baseline being properly controlled to ensure ongoing alignment with the business vision.

Solution Architecture Definition

The Solution Architecture Definition provides a high-level design framework for the solution. It is intended to cover both business and technical aspects of the solution to a level of detail that makes the scope of the solution clear but does not constrain evolutionary development.

Development Approach Definition

The Development Approach Definition provides a high-level definition of the tools, techniques, customs, practices and standards that will be applied to the evolutionary development of the solution. Importantly it describes how the quality of the solution will be assured. A strategy for testing and review is therefore a key part of the development approach and described in the Development Approach Definition.

Delivery Plan

The Delivery Plan provides a high-level schedule of Project Increments and, at least for the first/imminent Increment, Timeboxes that make up that Increment. It rarely deals with task-level detail unless there are tasks being carried out by people who are not part of the Solution Development Team or before the Solution Development Team is formed.

Management Approach Definition

The Management Approach Definition reflects the approach to the management of the project as a whole and considers, from a management perspective, how the project will be organised and planned, how stakeholders will be engaged in the project and how progress will be demonstrated and, if necessary, reported. The product is outlined in Feasibility and baselined at the end of Foundations and will only evolve beyond that when circumstances change or if review of the approach identifies areas for improvement.

Feasibility Assessment

The Feasibility Assessment provides a snapshot of the evolving business, solution and management products described above as they exist at the end of the Feasibility phase. The Feasibility Assessment may be expressed as a baselined collection of the products or as an executive summary covering the key aspects of each of them.

Foundation Summary

The Foundation Summary provides a snapshot of the evolving business, solution and management products described above as they exist at the end of the Foundations phase. The Foundation Summary may be expressed as a baselined collection of the products described above or as an executive summary covering the key aspects of each of them.

Evolving Solution

The Evolving Solution is made up of all appropriate components of the final solution together with any intermediate deliverables necessary to support development. At any given time, such components may be either complete, a baseline of a partial solution (a Solution Increment), or a work in progress. They include, where valuable: models, prototypes, supporting materials and testing and review artefacts.

At the end of each Project Increment the Solution Increment is deployed into live use and becomes the Deployed Solution.

Timebox Plan

The Timebox Plan elaborates on the objectives provided for that Timebox and details the deliverables of it, along with the activities to produce those deliverables and the resources to do the work.

The Timebox Plan is created by the Solution Development Team and is often represented on a Team Board as work to do, in progress, and done. It is updated at least on a daily basis at the Daily Stand-ups.

Timebox Review Record

The Timebox Review Record captures the feedback from each review that takes place during a Timebox. It describes what has been achieved up to that point together with any feedback that may influence plans moving forwards. Where appropriate, e.g. in a regulated environment, a formal auditable record of review comments from expert Business Advisors and other roles make this a governance product.

Project Review Report

The Project Review Report is typically a single document that is updated, incrementally, at the end of each Project Increment by the addition of new sections pertinent to that Increment.

At the end of each Project Increment, the purpose of this product is:

- To capture the feedback from the review of the delivered solution and to confirm what has been delivered and what has not
- To capture learning points from the retrospective for the Increment focussed on the process, practices employed and contributing roles and responsibilities
- Where appropriate to describe the business benefits that should now accrue through the proper use of the solution delivered by the project up to this point
- After the final Project Increment, as part of project closure, a retrospective covering the whole project is carried out that is partially informed by the records for each Project Increment.

Benefits Assessment

The Benefits Assessment describes how the benefits have actually accrued, following a period of use in live operation. For projects where benefits in the Business Case are expected to accrue over a prolonged period, it is possible that a number of Benefits Assessments may be produced on a periodic basis aligned with the timeframe used for justifying the investment.

Summary

It is important to remember DSDM values working solutions over comprehensive documentation. Many of the products identified above are documents and these should only be created where they add value to the project and/or the solution it creates or to provide an auditable record of how quality and compliance of the solution is assured.

It is as important to consider the form a product will take as it is to consider whether it will be created. Any product that is created must be fit for its intended purpose. That purpose and the value it represents needs to be clear to everybody involved. Without such clarity the product will have limited value and sometimes no value at all.

Project Planning and Control

In common with all other Agile methods DSDM values *responding to change over following a plan* but also sees *high-level* planning as critical to the success of a project. DSDM's high-level plans shape and structure the project and the work but do not get into the detail of exactly who does what and when.

Planning in DSDM starts with agreement of strategy – the approach to be taken to evolve the solution – and considers:

- Incremental delivery of the solution – breaking the project into Project Increments and Timeboxes
- Quality Assurance of the solution - how review and testing activity will be integrated into development

To address these considerations DSDM defines three Agile Project Planning Concepts, six Testing Concepts and four Tracking and Control concepts.

Planning Concepts

Outcome-based planning

Plans should reflect what should be delivered by when, rather than tasks needed to create the deliverables. It is important for a Project Manager to agree with a team what they will deliver by the end of a Timebox but it is equally important that the team is empowered to define and plan their own activity to achieve this.

Planning to sensible horizons at the right level of detail

Plans need to be realistic and robust. To achieve this, it is important to limit the number of assumptions on which plans are based. In general, the more you try to predict the future and the further into the detail you go, the more you rely on assumptions.

Plan and re-plan based on best available estimates

As the project progresses and the solution evolves, the understanding of what is needed to successfully complete the project becomes clearer. Plans should be subject to continual review and change based on this emerging clarity if they are to remain useful in predicting the future state of the project.

Testing Concepts

Testing integrated throughout

Early in a project, it is important to ensure that an agreed strategy for testing is in place. Testing activity should be as fully embedded as possible within the same Timebox as the development activity. This is because the earlier a defect is found, the easier and cheaper it is to fix. By the end of each Timebox the ideal outcome is for the Evolving Solution to be fully tested and business accepted although it is acknowledged that this is not always possible.

Collaborative Testing

Effective and productive testing involves the collaboration of all stakeholders on the project to increase the productivity of the test-fix-and-retest cycle.

Repeatable Testing

Since testing needs to support the DSDM principle to *"build incrementally from firm foundations"*, it is important that testing within a Timebox includes not only tests for the new features of the solution being built but where appropriate also tests for what has been built previously. It is therefore good practice to ensure tests are readily repeatable.

Prioritised Testing

As there is not always time to exhaustively test all aspects of the solution as it evolves, it is important to spend the time and effort that is available wisely. It may be helpful to prioritise testing on the basis of risk, i.e. on the likelihood of having introduced a defect and/or the impact of such a defect might have.

Independent Testing

A product should always be tested by someone other than its creator because it is as critical to test the understanding of a requirement as it is to test that the work done to fulfil that requirement was completed correctly. Active involvement of the Business Ambassador and Business Advisor roles in the project always provides an independent perspective for testing.

Test Driven Development

Using a Test-Driven approach, brought to prominence by eXtreme Programming (XP), the design and build of the test precedes development of the solution and helps define the requirement. The solution, or feature of it, is then developed until it passes all the specified tests. Research has shown that the practice of Test-Driven Development significantly increases the overall quality of the solution.

Tracking and Control Concepts

Timeboxing and Outcome-based measurement

The use of Timeboxes provides a structure of nested plans to support outcome-based measurement. Outcome-based measurement places the primary focus of measurement on what has been delivered. Understanding what has actually been delivered (the actual outcome) compared with what was planned provides the clearest possible indicator as to whether the project is on track.

Transparency of process and progress

At the Timebox level, transparency of process and progress comes from the use of a Team Board and the Daily Stand-up that should take place near the Team Board. In combination these make visible the necessary elements of control at the level of the Solution Development Team.

Responding to change

Following an approach where the detail of understanding of the problem and the detail of what makes up the solution is expected to emerge over time, it is essential that change is not only accepted as inevitable but that it is welcomed as part of the process of getting the solution right. That said, it is equally important: to maintain a *"focus on the business need"*; to *"deliver on time"*; and to *"never compromise quality"*. This means that change should also be controlled in order to maintain progress and for the solution to remain aligned with the business vision.

Management by exception

In the context of a DSDM project the Project Manager and the other project-level roles encourage an environment of empowerment for the Solution Development Team. Having agreed with the team what they Must, Should, and Could deliver by the end of the Timebox, the team members are expected to self-organise to achieve this. If for any reason the team feel they are unable to deliver what is expected (i.e. an exception occurs) they are expected to make this known to the Project Manager. The Project Manager and other project-level roles then take responsibility for managing the situation through to an appropriate resolution. Management by exception.

The DSDM Practices

Introduction

None of the practices described here are mandatory but they are all proven techniques that are recommended for use by the project team to help them fit practically and predictably into a governed, corporate project, programme or portfolio management environment without compromising project Agility.

MoSCoW Prioritisation used in conjunction with *Timeboxing* offers a truly effective way of ensuring predictability of delivery and to provide cost and timescale estimates at the end of Foundations that are both realistic and sustainable.

In addition, the *Timeboxing* practice provides a simple structured way that allows stakeholders beyond those directly involved with developing the solution (including those with a responsibility for ensuring compliance with regulatory or other standards) to review and influence the way the solution evolves.

Iterative Development requires all roles involved with the development of the solution to collaborate to get the solution right. Active involvement of business roles in the detail of development is essential.

Facilitated Workshops and *Modelling* represent practices that may be usefully employed in any project, Agile or otherwise. Both these practices promote and support communication and collaborative working.

The MoSCoW Prioritisation Practice

Delivering on a guaranteed date to a fixed cost means that some work originally planned for a delivery may have to be deferred. It may also be necessary to include work not originally identified.

Essential work must be completed and it is only less critical work that may be omitted from a delivery.

MoSCoW Prioritisation is a straightforward practice that helps to achieve this, with requirements prioritised according to the following MoSCoW rules:

- **Must Have:**
  Requirements that are fundamental to the solution. Without these the solution will be unworkable and useless. Must Haves define the Minimum Usable SubseT which a DSDM project guarantees to deliver
- **Should Have:**
  Important requirements for which there is a short-term workaround. Normally classed as mandatory when more time is available, but without them the overall business objective will still be broadly achieved
- **Could Have:**
  For requirements that can more easily be left out of the final solution because workarounds are relatively easy or cheap
- **Won't Have This Time:**
  For requirements that can be included in later timeframe. Won't Haves are excluded from plans for the current delivery

MoSCoW Prioritisation can provide the basis for decision making about project team activity at all levels. The advantage of MoSCoW is that it allows business expectations to be set at the project level, in the knowledge that the team will definitely deliver the Must Haves, they are likely to deliver most or all of the Should Haves, and they may deliver some Could Haves.

During the planning for the project in the Foundations phase, in order to ensure that the project delivers on time and on budget, a rule of thumb is to ensure that no more than 60% of the effort associated with the project is associated with Must Have requirements and that at least 20% of the effort is associated with Could Have requirements.

The Timeboxing Practice

DSDM defines a Timebox as a fixed period of time, at the end of which something complete and meaningful has been delivered. In DSDM, progress and success are measured by completion of products (requirements or other deliverables) rather than completing a series of tasks. Incremental delivery of the solution, Timebox-by-Timebox is the basis of measurement of progress and the basis of control for the project. By managing on-time/on-target delivery at the lowest level, on-time and on-target delivery at the higher levels can be assured.

The optimum length for a Timebox is typically between two and four weeks – long enough to achieve something useful, short enough to keep the Solution Development Team focused. In exceptional circumstances, a Timebox might be as long as six weeks.

DSDM recognises two styles of Timebox:

- A DSDM structured Timebox
- A free format Timebox

The DSDM Structured Timebox

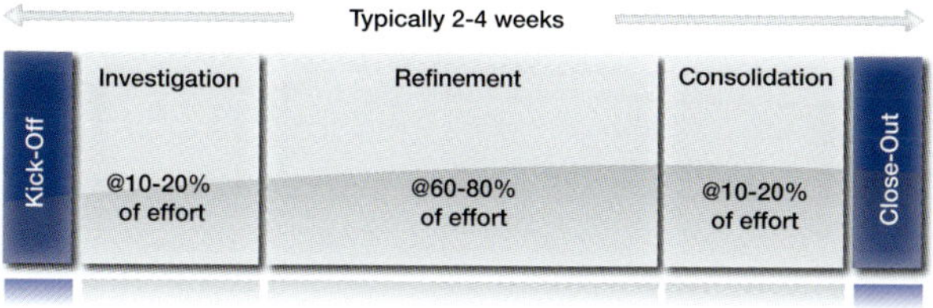

This is the original DSDM-style Timebox, which provides a standard, repeatable internal structure to a Timebox with opportunity for formal integrated feedback for governance and compliance purposes.

Kick-off

In the Kick-off session, the requirements to be addressed in the Timebox and their MoSCoW priority for that Timebox are negotiated and agreed.

Investigation

During the Investigation step, the Solution Development Team collaborates to achieve an understanding of the detail of all the requirements to be met and how they will be addressed as part of the Evolving Solution.

A quick (and, if required, formal) review at the end of the Investigation step provides an opportunity for the team to share their understanding of what will be done and their plans for doing it with those beyond the immediate team.

The Investigation step typically takes 10-20% of the Timebox duration and effort.

Refinement

During the Refinement step, the Solution Development Team (including Business Ambassadors and, where needed Business Advisors) work collaboratively to meet the requirements agreed in the Kick-off. The Evolving Solution is kept under constant informal review to ensure that it is evolving correctly to meet the business need. Testing activity is integrated into the iterative development of the solution to the greatest extent practical.

A quick (and, if required, formal) review at the end of the Refinement step provides an opportunity for the team to share their progress to date and to identify and plan the work of the

Consolidation step to ensure the highest priority items are fully complete and fit for purpose, meeting all required quality and acceptance criteria.

The Refinement step takes 60-80% of the Timebox duration and effort.

Consolidation

Work agreed at the end of the Refinement review is carried out together with any final work required to satisfy organisational or project standards. Final testing is completed and any deliverable failing to pass its tests or meet its pre-agreed acceptance criteria is not considered to be 'done'.

The Consolidation step typically takes 10-20% of the Timebox duration and effort.

Timebox Close-Out

The Timebox Close-out has two main objectives:

- A review and formal acceptance of the products delivered by the end of the Timebox and an understanding of anything that was included in the Kick-off but was not completed.

  The review often takes the form of a demonstration of the Evolving Solution delivered by the Solution Development Team.

  Anything planned for delivery but not actually delivered may be considered for inclusion in a later Timebox at the next planning session
- A Retrospective that considers the effectiveness of the collaborative, iterative development process and how it may be improved in future Timeboxes.

The Free Format Timebox

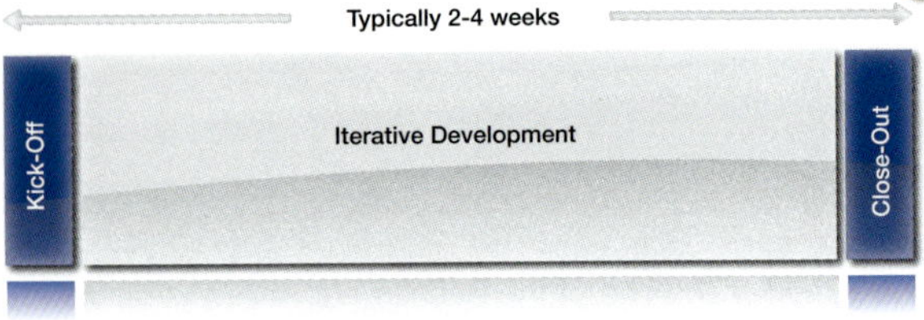

The free format Timebox reflects the style used by other popular Agile approaches such as a Scrum Sprint. A free format Timebox may be effective where the formality and structure of the DSDM structured Timebox is not possible or helpful.

The Kick-off and Close-out steps in the free format Timebox are exactly as described above for the structured Timebox.

Iterative Development of the deliverables agreed during the Kick-off is carried out in a single step as shown in the diagram above.

Using this approach, requirements are addressed in priority order and worked on sequentially until ideally they are fully complete or, less ideally until they are blocked either by other work within the Timebox or by external factors.

When using the free format Timebox it may be appropriate to apply the concepts of Investigation, Refinement and Consolidation with their associated, but probably less formal, reviews to each individual requirement to be addressed in order to keep a focus on meeting quality and acceptance criteria by the end of the Timebox and to facilitate on-going business engagement.

The Daily Stand-up

A key and integral part of all Timeboxes, regardless of the style adopted, is the Daily Stand-up. This is the Solution Development Team's opportunity to share information across the team and to do any day-to-day re-planning and reorganising necessary when issues occur.

On a daily basis, the Solution Development Team get together for a Stand-up session. The Stand-up usually takes place at the same time and same place each day (with the Timebox plan visible – typically in the form of a Team Board), so that others who are not part of the Solution Development Team may listen in. Normally facilitated by the Team Leader, the Stand-up is a daily opportunity for everyone to understand progress against objectives at a detailed level and to expose issues and blockers that may be getting in the way.

The Iterative Development Practice

Overview

Iterative Development is a process in which the Evolving Solution, or a part of it, evolves from a high-level concept to something with acknowledged business value.

Each cycle of the process is intended to bring the part of the solution being worked on closer to completion and is always a collaborative process, typically involving two or more members of the Solution Development Team.

Each cycle should:

- Be as short as possible, typically taking a day or two, with several cycles happening within a Timebox
- Be only as formal as it needs to be - in most cases limited to an informal cycle of Thought, Action and Conversation
- Involve the appropriate members of the Solution Development Team relevant to the work being done

Assuring Quality

One of the defining principles of DSDM is to *never compromise quality*. To achieve this, a required level of quality for the solution should be defined during the Feasibility and Foundations phases, early in the project lifecycle. During the Evolutionary Development phase continuous verification activity ensures that this level of quality is achieved. Verification may be *static* (a review) or *dynamic* (a test). In DSDM, review and testing activity is at the heart of the Iterative Development practice.

The Technical Coordinator for the project is responsible for the overall quality of the solution from a technical perspective and also for ensuring appropriate technical acceptance criteria for the solution are defined and subsequently met. The Technical Coordinator therefore needs to ensure that appropriate technical reviews are carried out and that testing is sufficiently comprehensive and rigorous to provide confidence that the solution created is fit for purpose.

The Solution Tester is responsible for carrying out all types of testing except for:

- Business acceptance testing: that is the responsibility of Business Ambassador(s) and Business Advisors
- Unit testing of the feature: that is the responsibility of the Solution Developer

As part of a collaborative team, the Solution Tester will support other roles in fulfilling their testing responsibilities by providing testing knowledge and expertise.

The Workshop Practice

Workshops are recommended because they encourage collaborative working and enable high quality team-based decisions to be made in a shortened timeframe. People brought together as a group communicate more effectively and generate more creative solutions.

A well-run Facilitated Workshop also delivers an outcome with a high degree of buy-in and ownership from those people who have taken part.

Ideally, workshops are facilitated by someone independent of the workshop result to ensure that all ideas and contributions are given equal weight. A trained facilitator creates an environment that allows full participation.

Effective workshops follow a well-defined and carefully thought-out process. As well as running the workshop on the day, this process includes defining and understanding the objective of the workshop, identifying appropriate participants, creating an agenda, managing the logistics and distributing any pre-reading to participants.

Facilitated Workshops are particularly valuable when applied to activities such as requirements identification and refinement, prioritisation, delivery or Timebox planning, risk analysis, problem solving, product reviews and retrospectives.

The Modelling Practice

Modelling is a practice for collaboratively evolving diagrams and pictures that define the problem or intended solution. Modelling is recommended because it helps improve communication through visualisation.

How often models are used and their formality depends on the nature of the project and the team's level of skill and experience in modelling techniques.

Models will also vary depending on the type of project, prevailing standards and best practice. In deciding what models should be created and when, the simplest rules to follow are:

- Be able to justify the value of the model for enhancing understanding of the given subject
- Use an approach that works for you and your organization
- Do enough and no more so that the purpose of the model is achieved

In DSDM, Prototyping extends the Modelling practice and involves the development of either evolutionary or disposable 'proof of concept' prototypes. A prototype is something created in the target technology to explore, prove or demonstrate how the solution should evolve. Prototypes are normally created where significant business or technical uncertainty exists around how a particular aspect of the solution should be evolved.

In Summary

The DSDM Agile Project Framework describes a robust, scalable and appropriately rigorous approach to solution development and delivery that is ideally suited to larger, more complex projects and/or larger, more complex or regulated organisations. The over-arching process framework along with the roles, products and practices have all evolved over time as part of DSDM and have been repeatedly proven in corporate environments. Far from being heavy and prescriptive, the framework is intended to provide a 'toolkit' for teams to make their lives simpler and easier and to provide transparency of progress and a demonstration of control to management and key project stakeholders. This is achieved by offering a fully Agile structure to support larger projects or projects in organisations where a more formal approach to project management and governance is needed.